THE
INDOOR
GRILLING
COOKBOOK

DEVELOPED BY

**WILLIAMS
SONOMA**

TEST KITCHEN

Photographs Erin Scott

weldon**owen**

CONTENTS

Spatchcocked Chicken with
Herb Butter & Grilled Garlic Heads (page 31)

Introducing Indoor Grilling

Outfit your kitchen with a stove-top grill pan or a countertop electric grill and you'll be serving grilled dishes any day of the year—in summer and winter, in sun and snow. Simple to use and easy to store, these no-fuss indoor grills provide consistent temperatures and optimal control for fast, even searing and cooking. That translates to meats, chicken, fish, vegetables, and fruits with perfectly caramelized exteriors and juicy, full of flavor interiors.

Stove-top grill pans are typically made of cast iron, have raised edges, and feature a ridged cooking surface that not only gives you the caramelized sear marks of an outdoor grill but also elevates the food above any drippings. They are designed to fit on a stove top over one or two burners, depending on the size and shape of the pan, and once they're smoking hot, they retain the heat, which helps guarantee even browning. Electric indoor grills sit comfortably on a countertop or table, heat quickly, sometimes come with interchangeable nonstick grids for different types of foods, have a below-grid tray to capture drippings, and promise nearly smoke-free grilling.

In these pages, you'll discover how to use these versatile specialty grills to create a variety of delicious and inspired dishes, including Rosemary-Garlic Lamb Chops with Hot Honey (page 37), Grilled Prawns with White Beans & Pesto (page 41), Grilled Whole Branzino with Lemons & Fresh Herbs (page 38), and Grilled Flatbreads with Burrata & Blistered Cherry Tomatoes (page 17). All the recipes that follow rely on just three easy-to-master steps—prep the ingredients, preheat the grill, then sear and cook—for turning out quick, easy, flavorful dishes. From kebabs to burgers, salads to stone fruit, indoor grilling will become your favorite go-to cooking method.

SMOKELESS
ELECTRIC GRILL
FEATURES

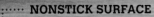

NONSTICK SURFACE
Dishwasher-safe nonstick grid
requires only a thin film of oil

DRIP TRAY
Drippings collect in an
easy-to-remove tray that
also helps prevent smoke

COMPACT SIZE
Fits comfortably on most
countertops or tables

EASY TO HANDLE
Wide handles are easy to grasp, even
when wearing heat-resistant mitts

STOVE-TOP GRILL PAN FEATURES

HEAVY CAST IRON
Readily absorbs and retains heat for perfect searing and even cooking

SHALLOW SIDES
Shallow sides, typically sloping, allow for easy maneuvering of foods

DESIGNED FOR STOVE TOPS
Depending on their size and shape, pans fit over one or two burners

RIDGED COOKING SURFACE
Pronounced ridges ensure classic grill marks and hold foods above their drippings

COLORFUL ACCENTS
Bright colors make pans attractive enough to go from stove to table

Aluminum foil packets not only make grilling individual servings easy—especially if the recipe calls for a sauce or syrup—but also simplify cleanup.

Tips for Indoor Grilling

Dreaming of a thick, juicy grilled burger or porterhouse steak on a cold, rainy night? With an indoor grill—stove top or electric—you can satisfy that craving rain or shine. Plus, these versatile grills mimic outdoor cooking with much less fuss. Here are some helpful tips to ensure success.

- To oil the pan or grid, select an oil with a high smoking point, such as canola, safflower, avocado, grapeseed, or light olive oil. Using tongs, dip a tightly crushed wad of paper towel into a small bowl of the oil, allowing the excess to drip off, then brush the hot cooking surface lightly and evenly with the saturated towel.

- Make sure the pan or grid is perfectly clean, then preheat fully before adding any ingredients to the cooking surface. This will take about 5 minutes for a stove-top pan. The pan is ready when you see a few light wisps of smoke—a signal the surface is hot enough to create grill marks. Alternatively, flick a few drops of water onto the hot surface; if they evaporate on contact, the pan is ready. For an electric grill, follow the manufacturer's directions for preheating.

- For even cooking, cut, slice, or shape foods so they are of uniform thickness.

- Once the food is on the hot surface, avoid moving it right away. Leaving it undisturbed for at least a minute ensures you'll get the desired grill marks, which add both flavor and visual appeal.

- Follow the recipe directions for when to flip the food. Most foods are flipped just once, and tongs are the ideal tool for this step. If the food seems to be charring too much before it's ready to flip, move or rotate it slightly. If the threat continues, flip the food ahead of the designated time or lower the heat a bit.

- For proper cleaning, following the instructions that came with your grill pan or electric grill. Most grill pans can be soaked in hot, soapy water and then wiped clean. If bits of food continue to stick, dislodge them with a firm-bristled nylon brush. Always dry your indoor grilling equipment thoroughly before storing.

Deconstructed Cobb Salad with Grilled Romaine, Tomatoes & Red Onion

A new look for an old favorite, this contemporary Cobb calls for lightly charred vegetables and Gorgonzola in place of the traditional Roquefort. To more closely match the classic, add grilled chicken breasts to the platter.

To make the dressing, in a frying pan over high heat, arrange the bacon slices in a single layer and cook, turning, until crispy, 3–4 minutes per side. Transfer to a paper towel–lined plate, reserving ¼ cup bacon fat in the pan. Let the bacon cool, then cut into thirds and set aside.

In a bowl, combine the shallot and vinegar and let stand for 5 minutes, then whisk in the mustard. Whisk in the olive oil and the reserved bacon fat. Season with salt and pepper. Set aside.

To make the salad, preheat a stove-top grill pan over medium-high heat, or preheat an electric indoor grill on medium-high heat. Brush with canola oil.

Meanwhile, in a small bowl, toss together the onion wedges and 1 tablespoon of the olive oil, and season with salt and pepper. In another small bowl, toss together the tomatoes and the remaining 1 tablespoon olive oil, and season with salt and pepper. Lightly brush the romaine with more olive oil.

Place the onion, tomatoes, and romaine, cut sides down, on separate areas of the grill. Cook, turning once, until the onion is charred and softened, the tomatoes are blistered and release their juices, and the romaine is slightly wilted and charred, about 10 minutes.

Transfer the romaine to a platter and arrange the reserved bacon, onion, tomatoes, avocado, and eggs around the romaine. Spoon the dressing over the salad. Top with the cheese, chives, and a few grindings of pepper and serve.

Serves 4

FOR THE DRESSING

½ lb sliced bacon

1 shallot, minced

¼ cup red wine vinegar

1 tablespoon Dijon mustard

¼ cup olive oil

Kosher salt and pepper

FOR THE SALAD

Canola oil as needed

1 red onion, cut into 8 wedges

2 tablespoons olive oil, plus more as needed

Kosher salt and pepper

1 cup cherry tomatoes, halved

2 large heads romaine lettuce, halved lengthwise

1 avocado, pitted, peeled, and sliced

2 hard-boiled eggs, peeled and halved lengthwise

½ cup crumbled Gorgonzola cheese

¼ cup chopped fresh chives

If you cannot find burrata, a rich semisoft cheese of soft curds and cream concealed in a "shell" of mozzarella, use fresh mozzarella in its place.

Grilled Flatbreads with Burrata & Blistered Cherry Tomatoes

For an eye-catching presentation, top this casual summertime main with a combination of cherry and grape tomatoes in a mix of colors, from red, yellow, and orange to mahogany brown and green. Accompany it with a green salad dressed with a balsamic vinaigrette and offer scoops of gelato for dessert.

Cut the pizza dough in half, shape into a ball, and let stand at room temperature for 1 hour. On a lightly floured surface, stretch each piece of dough into an oval about 12 inches long and 6 inches wide. Lightly dust with flour and cover with a kitchen towel until ready to use.

Preheat a stove-top grill pan over medium-high heat, or preheat an electric indoor grill on medium heat. Brush with canola oil.

In a small bowl, toss the tomatoes with enough olive oil to coat and season with salt and pepper. Place the tomatoes on the grill and cook, turning occasionally, until the tomatoes are blistered and release their juices, about 10 minutes. Return to the bowl.

Raise the heat to high. Brush the grill and both sides of the pizza dough with olive oil. Working with one piece at a time, place the dough on the grill and cook until deep golden brown, about 5 minutes. Turn the dough over and cook until deep golden brown on the other side and cooked through, about 5 minutes. Repeat with the remaining dough.

Transfer the flatbreads to a cutting board and top with the cheese and tomatoes. Drizzle with olive oil and vinegar, season with salt and pepper, and sprinkle with the basil. Cut into slices and serve.

Serves 2–4

1 lb pizza dough, homemade or store-bought

All-purpose flour, for dusting

½ lb cherry tomatoes, halved

Canola oil as needed

Olive oil as needed

Kosher salt and pepper

½ lb burrata cheese

Balsamic vinegar, for drizzling

1 cup loosely packed fresh basil leaves, thinly sliced

Grilled Little Gems & Radishes with Cashew Caesar Dressing

In this vegan take on a classic Caesar dressing, the traditional egg yolks, cheese, and anchovies have been swapped out in favor of cashews, nut milk, and capers. If you cannot find Little Gem lettuces, romaine lettuce hearts, halved and grilled as directed, can take their place.

To make the dressing, in a Vitamix or other high-powered blender, combine the cashews, garlic, almond milk, lemon juice, capers, mustard, maple syrup, and sea salt and blend on high speed until just combined. With the blender running on low speed, slowly pour in **the** avocado oil, then blend on high speed until the dressing is completely smooth. Set aside.

Preheat a stove-top grill pan over medium-high heat, or preheat an electric indoor grill on medium-high heat. Brush with avocado oil.

Meanwhile, brush the lettuce with olive oil. In a small bowl, toss the radishes with enough olive oil to coat. Season the lettuce and radishes with salt and pepper.

Place the radishes, cut sides down, on the grill and cook until tender, about 7 minutes. Turn the radishes over and cook until they are just tender but still retain a little crunch, about 7 minutes. Meanwhile, place the lettuce, cut sides down, on the grill and cook until nicely charred, about 5 minutes. Turn the lettuce over and cook until grill marked on the other side, 2–3 minutes. Transfer to a plate and let cool slightly, then separate the leaves.

Transfer the lettuce leaves to a serving bowl or platter and top with the radishes and pepitas. Drizzle with the dressing (reserve any extra for another use). Add a squeeze of lemon juice, sprinkle lightly with flaky sea salt, and serve.

Serves 4

FOR THE DRESSING

1 cup raw cashews, soaked overnight or in boiled water for 30 minutes until softened, then drained

2 cloves garlic, peeled

½ cup unsweetened almond milk or other nut milk

2 tablespoons lemon juice

1 tablespoon capers

1 teaspoon Dijon mustard

1 teaspoon pure maple syrup

1 teaspoon kosher salt

½ cup avocado oil, plus more as needed

Olive oil as needed

4 heads Little Gem lettuce, halved lengthwise

8 radishes, trimmed and halved lengthwise

Kosher salt and pepper

¼ cup pepitas, roasted

½ lemon

Flaky sea salt

Grilled Summer Squash with Goat Cheese, Hazelnuts & Mint

Choose small, firm summer squash—zucchini, straight or crookneck yellow, pattypan, Zephyr—for grilling, and serve them fresh off the heat, as here, or at room temperature. Other cheese and nut combos, such as crumbled feta or ricotta salata with toasted walnuts or pine nuts, will also complement the squash.

Preheat a stove-top grill pan over high heat, or preheat an electric indoor grill on high heat. Brush with canola oil.

Meanwhile, lightly brush the squash on both sides with olive oil. Season with kosher salt and pepper.

Place the squash on the grill and cook, turning every few minutes, until charred and tender, 6–8 minutes total.

Transfer the squash to a platter and garnish with the cheese, hazelnuts, and mint leaves. Lightly drizzle with olive oil, sprinkle with flaky sea salt, and serve.

Serves 4

Canola oil as needed

4 summer squash (about 1 lb total), halved lengthwise

Olive oil as needed

Kosher salt and freshly ground pepper

¼ cup crumbled goat cheese

¼ cup roasted hazelnuts, crushed

¼ cup fresh mint leaves

Flaky sea salt

Za'atar-Grilled Eggplant with Tahini, Pomegranate & Walnuts

Long, narrow Chinese or shorter, slender Japanese eggplants are particularly well suited to grilling. Because they have thinner skin and fewer seeds than globe or Italian eggplants, their flesh turns out extra creamy. If you're pressed for time, substitute plain yogurt for the tahini sauce.

To make the tahini sauce, in a bowl, whisk together the water, tahini, oil, and lemon juice. Season with salt and pepper. Set aside.

Using a sharp knife, score the flesh side of the eggplant halves with 3 diagonal lines going in each direction to form a diamond pattern. Brush the eggplants on both sides with the olive oil, allowing it to be absorbed into the flesh. Season with the za'atar, salt, and pepper.

Preheat a stove-top grill pan over high heat, or preheat an electric indoor grill on high heat. Brush with canola oil.

Place the eggplants, cut sides down, on the grill and cook until tender and lightly charred, about 5 minutes. Turn the eggplants over and cook until they look slightly deflated and the skin is charred, 5–7 minutes.

Transfer the eggplants to a platter. Drizzle with pomegranate molasses and sprinkle with the walnuts, pomegranate seeds, and za'atar. Garnish with mint and serve with the tahini sauce.

Serves 4–6

FOR THE TAHINI SAUCE

1 cup water

½ cup tahini

3 tablespoons olive oil

2 tablespoons fresh lemon juice

Kosher salt and pepper

Canola oil as needed

2 large Asian eggplants, halved lengthwise

⅓ cup olive oil

2 tablespoons za'atar, plus more for garnish

Kosher salt and pepper

Canola oil as needed

Pomegranate molasses, for drizzling

½ cup walnuts, toasted and chopped

½ cup pomegranate seeds

Fresh mint leaves, for garnish

Teriyaki Cauliflower Steaks with Sesame Gremolata

Because it contains sugar, teriyaki sauce tends to scorch, so keep a watchful eye and lower the heat if needed. If your grill pan is small, cook the cauliflower in two batches, keeping the first batch warm while the second one cooks.

To make the teriyaki sauce, in a saucepan over medium heat, combine the 1 cup water, soy sauce, brown sugar, garlic, and ginger and bring to a simmer, stirring to dissolve the sugar, then simmer for 5 minutes. Meanwhile, in a small bowl, whisk together the 2 tablespoons water and cornstarch until smooth. Whisk into the teriyaki sauce until combined. Remove the pan from the heat and continue to whisk until the sauce thickens, about 30 seconds. Set aside.

To make the sesame gremolata, in a small bowl, stir together the olive oil, sesame oil, lime juice, garlic, cilantro, and sesame seeds. Season with salt and pepper. Set aside.

Trim the stem end from the cauliflower but leave it intact. Place the cauliflower, stem side down, on the cutting board and cut into four 1-inch slices. Generously brush on both sides with olive oil.

Preheat a stove-top grill pan over high heat, or preheat an electric indoor grill on high heat.

Place the cauliflower steaks on the grill and cook, turning once, until charred and tender, about 4 minutes per side, brushing with the teriyaki sauce halfway through cooking. If the sauce begins to burn, reduce the heat.

Transfer the cauliflower steaks to a platter and brush with any remaining teriyaki sauce. Garnish with sesame seeds and serve with the gremolata.

Serves 4

FOR THE TERIYAKI SAUCE

1 cup plus 2 tablespoons water

½ cup soy sauce

¼ cup firmly packed light brown sugar

2 cloves garlic, minced

1 teaspoon grated peeled fresh ginger

2 tablespoons cornstarch

FOR THE SESAME GREMOLATA

¼ cup olive oil

2 tablespoons toasted sesame oil

Juice of 1 lime

1 clove garlic, minced

1 cup chopped fresh cilantro

2 tablespoons toasted sesame seeds, plus more for garnish

Kosher salt and pepper

1 large head cauliflower
Olive oil as needed

Grilled Artichokes with Charred Lemons & Aioli

Grilling lends flavor but not much tenderness to artichokes, so be sure they are cooked nearly enough to eat before they hit the grill pan. To save time the day of serving, boil them up to a day in advance and refrigerate them.

Bring a large pot of water to a boil over high heat. Squeeze 2 of the lemon halves over the artichokes. Add the artichokes to the boiling water and cook until tender when pierced with a knife, about 15 minutes. Transfer to a cutting board and let cool slightly, then scoop out and discard the choke.

Preheat a stove-top grill pan over high heat, or preheat an electric indoor grill on high heat. Brush with canola oil.

Meanwhile, drizzle the artichoke halves with olive oil, squeeze 2 more lemon halves over them, and season with salt and pepper.

Place the artichokes on the grill and cook, turning once, until charred and softened, 15–20 minutes.

Meanwhile, make the lemon-garlic aioli: In a small bowl, stir together the mayonnaise, lemon zest and juice, and garlic. Season with salt and pepper. Set aside.

When the artichokes are almost done, place the remaining 4 lemon halves, cut sides down, on the grill and cook until charred, about 5 minutes.

Transfer the artichokes and grilled lemons to a platter and garnish with parsley leaves. Serve with the lemon-garlic aioli for dipping.

Serves 4

4 lemons, halved crosswise

3 artichokes, tops trimmed and artichokes halved lengthwise

Canola oil as needed

Olive oil as needed

Kosher salt and pepper

FOR THE LEMON-GARLIC AIOLI

1 cup mayonnaise

Zest and juice of 1 lemon

3 cloves garlic, grated

Kosher salt and pepper

Fresh flat-leaf parsley leaves, for garnish

Charred Broccolini with Dill & Toasted Almonds

If your market is out of broccolini, purchase broccoli crowns, quarter them lengthwise, and grill them the same way. This easy side dish is an excellent accompaniment to grilled meats or fish or simple seafood pastas.

Preheat a stove-top grill pan over medium-high heat, or preheat an electric indoor grill on medium-high heat. Brush with canola oil.

Meanwhile, place the broccolini on a baking sheet, lightly drizzle with olive oil, and season with salt and pepper.

Place the broccolini on the grill and cook until charred, about 5 minutes. Turn the broccolini over and cook until charred on the other side and just tender, 2–3 minutes.

Transfer the broccolini to a platter and drizzle with balsamic vinegar. Garnish with the dill and almonds, sprinkle with flaky sea salt and a few grindings of pepper, and serve.

Serves 2–4

Canola oil as needed

1 bunch broccolini, halved lengthwise

Olive oil as needed

Kosher salt and pepper

Balsamic vinegar, for drizzling

½ cup dill fronds

¼ cup sliced almonds, toasted

Flaky sea salt, for serving

To develop a deeper flavor and a better char, brush the kebabs as they cook with a mixture of ¼ cup honey and 1–2 tablespoons Sriracha sauce.

Sriracha, Honey & Sesame Beef Kebabs with Bok Choy

A sweet-sour-hot-salty marinade infuses these beef cubes with bold flavors, especially if they're allowed to marinate overnight. Don't skip the jasmine rice, as it makes a great bed for the kebabs, soaking up all the flavorful juices.

Place the beef in a large lock-top plastic bag. In a small bowl, whisk together the honey, vinegar, Sriracha, fish sauce, sesame oil, and garlic. Pour the marinade into the bag with the beef, seal the bag, and toss to coat the meat. Refrigerate for at least 30 minutes or up to overnight. Let the beef stand at room temperature for 30 minutes before assembling the skewers.

If using wooden skewers, soak 4 skewers in water for 30 minutes and then drain.

Place the bok choy halves in a bowl, lightly drizzle with sesame oil, and toss to coat. Season with salt and pepper.

Remove the beef from the marinade. Working with 1 skewer at a time, skewer 1 piece of beef and 1 piece of bok choy, leaving about 1 inch of space at the bottom of the skewer. Repeat so there are 4 pieces of beef on the skewer.

Preheat a stove-top grill pan over high heat, or preheat an electric indoor grill on high heat. Brush with canola oil.

When the grill is almost smoking, working in batches if needed, place the kebabs on the grill and cook, turning once, until the beef is charred and cooked to your liking, 4–5 minutes per side for medium-rare.

Transfer the kebabs to a platter and let rest for 10 minutes. Garnish with the green onion, black sesame seeds, and Thai basil. Serve with jasmine rice, if desired.

Serves 4

2 lb beef tri-tip or sirloin, cut into 2-inch cubes

¼ cup honey

2 tablespoons rice vinegar

1 tablespoon Sriracha

1 tablespoon fish sauce

1 tablespoon toasted sesame oil, plus more as needed

2 cloves garlic, grated

4 heads baby bok choy, cut in half lengthwise, green leaves loosened from sturdier white part

Kosher salt and pepper

Canola oil as needed

1 green onion, both white and pale green parts, thinly sliced

Black sesame seeds, for garnish

Fresh Thai basil, for garnish

Steamed jasmine rice, for serving (optional)

Spiced Chicken Kebabs with Grilled Plantains & Mango-Lime Salsa

In this Latin-inspired dish, richly spiced chicken is paired with naturally sweet plantains, which char and caramelize quickly on a hot grill pan. Make sure the plantains are ripe—the skin mostly black, signaling the starches have converted to sugars—before grilling.

To make the kebabs, place the chicken in a large lock-top plastic bag. In a small bowl, whisk together the brown sugar, garlic, thyme, allspice, cinnamon, cayenne, 1 teaspoon salt, and ½ teaspoon black pepper. Whisk in the olive oil and lime juice. Pour the marinade into the bag with the chicken, seal the bag, and toss to coat the meat. Refrigerate for at least 3 hours or up to overnight. Let the chicken stand at room temperature for 30 minutes before assembling the skewers.

Meanwhile, make the mango-lime salsa: In a medium bowl, stir together the mangoes, onion, lime juice, thyme, garlic, orange zest, 1½ teaspoons salt, and black pepper to taste. Cover and refrigerate until ready to serve. (The longer the salsa sits, the more the flavors will develop.) Bring to room temperature before serving.

If using wooden skewers, soak 6 skewers in water for 30 minutes and then drain.

Remove the chicken from the marinade (discard the marinade). Thread the chicken onto the skewers, using 4–6 pieces per skewer.

FOR THE KEBABS

2 lb skinless, boneless chicken thighs, cut into 2-inch pieces

2 tablespoons firmly packed light brown sugar

2 teaspoons minced garlic

2 teaspoons minced fresh thyme

1 teaspoon ground allspice

½ teaspoon ground cinnamon

¼ teaspoon cayenne pepper

Kosher salt and pepper

2 tablespoons olive oil

2 tablespoons fresh lime juice

Preheat a stove-top grill pan over high heat, or preheat an electric indoor grill on high heat. Brush with canola oil.

When the grill is almost smoking, working in batches if needed, place the kebabs on the grill and cook, turning once, until the chicken is charred and cooked through, about 10 minutes per side. Transfer to a platter.

Meanwhile, brush the plantains on both sides with canola oil, sprinkle with the brown sugar, and season with salt and black pepper. Brush the grill with canola oil. Place the plantains on the grill and cook, turning once, until lightly charred, about 30 seconds per side. Transfer to the platter with the kebabs.

Serve the kebabs and plantains with the mango-lime salsa and a side of black beans, if desired.

Serves 6

FOR THE MANGO-LIME SALSA

3 mangoes, pitted, peeled, and diced

½ red onion, minced

5 tablespoons fresh lime juice

1 tablespoon fresh thyme leaves

1 teaspoon minced garlic

Grated zest of 1 orange

Kosher salt and pepper

Canola oil as needed

4 ripe plantains, peeled and cut on the diagonal into ½-inch slices

2 tablespoons firmly packed light brown sugar

Kosher salt and pepper

Cooked black beans, for serving (optional)

For extra lemony flavor, spritz the cut chicken with the grilled lemon halves just before serving.

Spatchcocked Chicken with Herb Butter & Grilled Garlic Heads

Spatchcocking—splitting a bird and removing the backbone so it will lie flat—yields faster, more even cooking and crispier skin. It's a great choice for indoor grilling, as the bird absorbs flavors better and turns out juicer than chicken pieces.

Preheat the oven to 400°F.

Cut off the top of the garlic heads to expose the cloves. Place each on a separate sheet of aluminum foil and lightly drizzle with olive oil. Loosely close the foil and roast until the garlic is just tender, about 30 minutes. Let cool.

Meanwhile, in a small bowl, stir together the butter, oregano, thyme, tarragon, lemon zest, and grated garlic until well combined. Season the chicken with salt and pepper. Using your hands, rub the herb butter over and under the skin.

Preheat a stove-top grill pan over medium-high heat, or preheat an electric indoor grill on medium-high heat. Brush with oil.

Place the chicken, breast side down, on the grill and cook for about 15 minutes. Turn the chicken over and cook until the skin is golden and crisp and an instant-read thermometer inserted into the thickest part of the thigh or breast registers 165°F, about 15 minutes. If the chicken is not yet done, continue cooking, turning every few minutes, until the desired internal temperature is reached. Transfer the chicken to a cutting board and let rest for 10 minutes.

Meanwhile, place the garlic heads and lemon halves, cut sides down, on the grill and cook until charred, about 5 minutes. Transfer to the cutting board.

Cut the chicken into serving pieces and garnish with flaky sea salt, oregano, thyme, and tarragon.

Serves 4

2 heads garlic

Olive oil as needed

½ cup unsalted butter, at room temperature

1 tablespoon fresh oregano, roughly chopped, plus more for garnish

1 tablespoon fresh thyme, roughly chopped, plus more for garnish

1 tablespoon fresh tarragon, roughly chopped, plus more for garnish

Grated zest of 1 lemon

2 cloves garlic, grated

Canola oil as needed

1 whole chicken (about 4 lb), spatchcocked

Kosher salt and pepper

2 lemons, halved crosswise

Flaky sea salt, for serving

Grilled Pork Chops, Peaches & Fennel with Feta

If your grill pan is too small to accommodate the chops, peaches, and fennel at the same time, cook the chops first, tent them, and then cook the peaches and fennel. Your favorite white or yellow peach—or even nectarine—will work here.

In a small bowl, stir together the mustard, ground fennel, granulated garlic, 2 teaspoons salt, and 1 teaspoon pepper. Rub the mixture on both sides of the pork chops. Cover and refrigerate for at least 1 hour or up to overnight. Let the pork chops stand at room temperature for 30 minutes before grilling.

In a small bowl, stir together the basil and olive oil, and season with salt and pepper. Set aside.

In a bowl, combine the peaches and fennel, drizzle with olive oil, and toss to coat. Season lightly with salt and pepper.

Preheat a stove-top grill pan over high heat, or preheat an electric indoor grill on high heat. Brush with canola oil.

Place the pork chops on the grill and cook, turning once, until nicely grill marked and an instant-read thermometer inserted into the center of the chops, away from the bone, registers 145°F, about 6 minutes per side, or until done to your liking. During the last 5 minutes of cooking, place the peaches and fennel on the grill and cook until lightly charred and softened, about 10 minutes.

Transfer the pork chops to a platter or cutting board while the peaches and fennel finish cooking. Arrange the chops, peaches, fennel, and cheese on a platter. Drizzle with the basil oil, garnish with basil leaves and fennel fronds, and serve.

Serves 4

3 tablespoons Dijon mustard

2 teaspoons ground fennel seeds

2 teaspoons granulated garlic

Kosher salt and pepper

4 thick-cut, bone-in pork chops, each 1 ½ inches thick (about 4 lb total)

1 cup fresh basil leaves, minced, plus whole leaves for garnish

½ cup olive oil, plus more as needed

Canola oil as needed

4 peaches, pitted and quartered

1 large fennel bulb, trimmed and cut into 8 wedges, fronds reserved for garnish

6 oz feta cheese, cut into slices

Most pork bred today is very lean. For more flavorful, jucier kebabs, look for heritage breeds, such as Duroc or Berkshire.

Rosemary-Garlic Pork Kebabs with Grilled Fingerlings & Watercress

Potatoes are a natural for grilling, turning out lightly charred on the exterior and creamy and delicious in the interior. Here, fingerlings are used, but small red potatoes would also be good with these rosemary-infused pork kebabs.

In a large bowl, whisk together the olive oil, honey, lemon juice, rosemary, garlic, fennel seeds, and red pepper flakes. Reserve ½ cup of the marinade. Season the pork with salt and pepper. Add the pork to the bowl with the remaining marinade and toss to coat. Cover and refrigerate for at least 1 hour or up to 8 hours. Let the pork stand at room temperature for 30 minutes before assembling the skewers.

Remove the pork from the marinade. Thread the pork onto the skewers, leaving about 1 inch of space at the bottom and top of the skewers. In a bowl, toss the potatoes with enough oil to lightly coat and season with salt and pepper.

Preheat a stove-top grill pan over medium-high heat, or preheat an electric indoor grill on medium-high heat. Brush with canola oil.

When the grill is almost smoking, place the kebabs on the grill and cook, turning once and basting them with the reserved marinade, until the pork is charred and the internal temperature reaches 145°F, 8-10 minutes per side. Transfer the kebabs to a platter and drizzle with olive oil.

Place the potatoes, cut sides down, on the grill and cook, turning occasionally, until charred and tender, about 10 minutes. Transfer to the platter with the kebabs and season with flaky sea salt. Arrange the watercress alongside and serve.

Serves 8

½ cup olive oil, plus more as needed

1 tablespoon honey

1 tablespoon fresh lemon juice

Leaves from 8 fresh rosemary sprigs, minced

4 cloves garlic, minced

1 teaspoon fennel seeds, toasted

½ teaspoon red pepper flakes

2 lb boneless pork loin, cut into 1-inch pieces

Kosher salt and pepper

8 wooden skewers, soaked in water for 30 minutes and drained

Canola oil as needed

1 lb fingerling potatoes, halved lengthwise

Flaky sea salt

2 bunches watercress, tough stems removed

Grilled Kielbasa & Pineapple with Fennel Slaw

Both the smoky kielbasa and the naturally sweet pineapple call for less than 10 minutes on a hot grill pan. Swabbing them with the sweet-hot basting sauce as they cook contributes flavor and helps to caramelize the pineapple.

In a small saucepan over medium-high heat, combine the pineapple juice, chili powder, brown sugar, and a pinch of salt and bring to a boil. Reduce the heat to low and simmer, stirring occasionally, until the mixture is reduced by about half, about 15 minutes. Remove from the heat.

Preheat a stove-top grill pan over high heat, or preheat an electric indoor grill on high heat. Brush with canola oil.

Working in batches if needed, place the sausage and pineapple on the grill. Cook, turning once and basting the sausage with the pineapple juice mixture, until the sausage is warmed through and the skin is blistered and charred, and the pineapple is tender and charred, about 4 minutes per side.

Transfer the sausage and pineapple to a platter and drizzle the sausage with any remaining pineapple juice mixture. Serve with the fennel slaw and spicy mustard.

Serves 4

1 cup pineapple juice

1 teaspoon chili powder

3 tablespoons firmly packed light brown sugar

Kosher salt

Canola oil as needed

1½ lb kielbasa sausage

1 pineapple, peeled, cored, and cut crosswise into ¼-inch-thick slices

Fennel Slaw (page 46)

Spicy whole-grain mustard, for serving

Rosemary-Garlic Lamb Chops with Hot Honey

Lamb loin and lamb rib chops are both very tender, but rib chops typically have more marbling, which yields a juicier, more flavorful grilled finish. If you want to keep the heat down, choose a milder chile, such as a jalapeño, New Mexico, or Anaheim.

In a large bowl, whisk together the olive oil, rosemary, and garlic. Season the lamb chops generously with salt and pepper. Add the chops to the marinade and turn to coat. Cover and refrigerate for at least 1 hour or up to 8 hours. Let the lamb chops stand at room temperature for 30 minutes before grilling.

Preheat a stove-top grill pan over high heat, or preheat an electric indoor grill on high heat. Brush with canola oil.

Remove the lamb chops from the marinade (discard the marinade). Working in batches if needed, place the chops on the grill and cook, turning once, until nicely grill marked and an instant-read thermometer inserted into the center of the chops, away from the bone, registers 130°F for medium-rare, about 4 minutes per side, or until done to your liking.

Meanwhile in a small saucepan over medium-low heat, combine the honey and chile peppers and bring to a simmer. Cook, stirring occasionally, until the honey is melted and the peppers just begin to turn dark green and glossy, about 10 minutes.

Transfer the lamb chops to a serving platter and arrange the watercress alongside. Drizzle the hot honey over the chops and serve.

Serves 4

1 cup olive oil

¼ cup chopped fresh rosemary

8 cloves garlic, minced

2 lb lamb rib or loin chops

Kosher salt and pepper

Canola oil as needed

1 cup honey

2 chile peppers, seeded and thinly sliced

1 bunch watercress, tough stems removed

Grilled Branzino with Lemons & Fresh Herbs

If you cannot find branzino, small black bass or red snapper makes a good substitute. Be sure to score the fish as directed, as it helps distribute the heat more evenly. Romaine lettuce hearts, halved lengthwise, drizzled with olive oil, and grilled, cut side down, for a minute or so, will complement the fish.

Using a sharp knife, lightly score the skin on both sides of the fish from the fin to the underbelly. Rub a generous amount of oil all over the skin and inside the cavity, and season with salt and pepper. Fill the cavity with the lemon slices, parsley, and dill.

Preheat a stove-top grill pan over high heat, or preheat an electric indoor grill on high heat. Brush with canola oil.

Place the fish on the grill and cook until the skin is charred, about 6 minutes. Carefully turn the fish over and cook until the inside of the fish is opaque, about 7 minutes. Halfway through cooking, remove the lemon slices from the fish cavity, place them directly on the grill, and cook, turning once, until charred, about 3 minutes per side.

Transfer the branzino to a platter and serve with the charred lemons.

Serves 2

2 whole branzino (about 1–1½ lbs each), cleaned, rinsed, and patted dry

Olive oil as needed

Kosher salt and pepper

2 lemons, thinly sliced

6 fresh flat-leaf parsley sprigs

6 fresh dill sprigs

Canola oil as needed

Lobster Tails with Tarragon Butter

To butterfly each lobster tail, using kitchen shears and starting at the open end, cut along the center of the top shell, stopping at the tail fins. Using a knife and tracing the shell cut line, cut through the meat, stopping short of the bottom shell. Gently pull the top shell open like a book, exposing the meat.

In a small bowl, stir together the butter, tarragon, and garlic until well combined. Season with pepper. Transfer the butter mixture to a small saucepan, set over medium heat, and heat, stirring occasionally, until melted, about 2–3 minutes.

Preheat a stove-top grill pan over medium-high heat, or preheat an electric indoor grill on medium-high heat. Brush with canola oil.

Meanwhile, place the lobster tails on a baking sheet, season generously with salt, and brush with some of the melted butter.

When the grill is almost smoking, place the lobster tails, cut sides down, on the grill and cook until charred, about 2 minutes. Turn the tails over, brush with a little melted butter, and cook for about 5 minutes. Turn the tails over again and cook until the lobster meat is opaque, about 5 minutes longer.

Transfer the lobster tails to a platter, add a few grindings of pepper, and garnish with tarragon leaves. Serve with the lemon wedges and remaining melted butter.

Serves 4

½ cup unsalted butter, at room temperature

Leaves from 5 fresh tarragon sprigs, roughly chopped, plus whole leaves for garnish

2 cloves garlic, minced

Kosher salt and pepper

Canola oil as needed

4 lobster tails, butterflied (see note)

1 lemon, cut into wedges

Prawns with White Beans & Pesto

This simple yet satisfying dish needs only a green salad and a chilled Vermentino to transport you to an Italian seaside trattoria. Choose large prawns for grilling and avoid high heat, which can too easily lead to overcooking. For extra lemony flavor, squeeze an additional lemon over the prawns before grilling.

To make the pesto, in a food processor, combine the pine nuts and garlic and pulse until roughly chopped. Add the basil and parsley sprigs and pulse until chopped. With the processor running on low speed, slowly pour in the olive oil and process until the oil is combined. Add the Parmesan, pecorino, lemon juice, and a few pinches each of salt and pepper and process until blended. Transfer to a bowl and set aside.

In a saucepan over medium heat, warm enough canola oil to lightly coat the bottom of the pan. Add the garlic and cook, stirring occasionally, until fragrant and lightly browned, about 3 minutes. Add enough broth to cover the garlic and reach halfway up the sides of the pan. Bring to a simmer and cook, stirring occasionally, until the broth is reduced by about half, about 5 minutes. Stir in the white beans; the consistency should be loose but not soupy. Set aside.

Preheat a stove-top grill pan over medium-high heat, or preheat an electric indoor grill on medium-high heat. Brush with canola oil.

Meanwhile, in a large bowl, toss together the prawns, olive oil, and a few pinches each of salt and pepper.

When the grill is almost smoking, place the prawns on the grill and cook, turning once, until opaque, about 10 minutes.

Transfer the white beans to a serving bowl, top with the prawns, and drizzle with the pesto. Garnish with lemon zest, a squeeze of lemon juice, and parsley leaves and serve.

Serves 4

FOR THE PESTO

¼ cup pine nuts

2 cloves garlic, peeled

3 cups fresh basil leaves

1 cup fresh flat-leaf parsley sprigs, plus leaves for garnish

½ cup olive oil

½ cup grated Parmesan cheese

¼ cup grated pecorino cheese

Juice of ½ lemon

Kosher salt and pepper

Canola oil as needed

4 cloves garlic, smashed

Chicken broth as needed

2 cups cooked white beans

2 lb head-on, tail-on prawns, peeled and deveined

1 tablespoon olive oil

Kosher salt and pepper

Grated lemon zest and fresh lemon juice, for garnish

Serve these savory kebabs with warmed pita bread. If you can't find labneh, whole-milk Greek yogurt makes a good substitute.

Salmon Kebabs with Zucchini, Herbed Labneh & Harissa

Salmon kebabs are a perfect lean protein for indoor grilling. To ensure the fish chunks hold together, oil the grill and get it smoking hot before adding the kebabs, then don't move them unnecessarily, turning them only once. Look for labneh, a creamy, yogurt-based Middle Eastern cheese, in specialty markets.

To make the kebabs, if using wooden skewers, soak 8 skewers in water for 30 minutes and then drain.

Thread the salmon, zucchini, and a few pieces of onion onto the skewers, alternating the ingredients and using about 4 pieces of salmon per skewer. Transfer to a baking sheet. Drizzle the kebabs with olive oil and season with salt and pepper.

To make the herbed labneh, in a small bowl, stir together the labneh, oregano, parsley, mint, and lemon juice. Season with salt and pepper. Set aside.

To make the harissa, in another small bowl, stir together the harissa and olive oil. Set aside.

Preheat a stove-top grill pan over medium-high heat, or preheat an electric indoor grill on medium-high heat. Brush with canola oil.

When the grill is almost smoking, working in batches if needed, place the kebabs on the grill and cook, turning once, until the salmon is charred and cooked through to your liking and the vegetables are just tender, 3–5 minutes per side.

Transfer the kebabs to a platter and serve with the herbed labneh and harissa.

Serves 8

FOR THE KEBABS

2 lb salmon fillets, cut into 1-inch pieces (skin removed, if desired)

2 zucchini, cut into ¼-inch-thick rounds

1 yellow onion, cut into 1-inch pieces

Olive oil as needed

Kosher salt and pepper

FOR THE HERBED LABNEH

1 cup labneh

1 tablespoon each chopped fresh oregano and chopped fresh flat-leaf parsley

2 teaspoons chopped fresh mint

Juice from 1 lemon

Kosher salt and pepper

FOR THE HARISSA

3 tablespoons harissa

2 tablespoons olive oil

Canola oil as needed

Mushroom Burgers with Smashed Avocado & Spicy Pickled Carrots

Packed with flavor and nutrients, these hearty vegetarian burgers boast the ideal ratio of mushrooms to binders—eggs, panko, and rice—to ensure they hold together when flipped on the grill pan. If you like, swap out the sesame seed buns for whole-wheat buns.

To make the pickled carrots, in a medium bowl, stir together the carrots and jalapeño. In a small saucepan over medium-high heat, combine the water, white wine vinegar, rice vinegar, sugar, and 1 teaspoon salt and bring to a simmer, stirring to dissolve the sugar and salt. Pour over the carrots and jalapeño and refrigerate until cool.

To make the mushroom burgers, in a food processor, pulse the mushrooms until coarsely chopped and transfer to a medium bowl. In a small bowl, whisk together the soy sauce, vinegar, and chile paste. Set aside.

In a sauté pan over medium heat, warm the sesame oil. Add the ginger and garlic and cook, stirring, until fragrant, about 1 minute. Add the mushrooms and cook, stirring, until coated, 1-2 minutes. Add the soy sauce mixture and cook, stirring occasionally, until the mushrooms are tender and the sauce has thickened, 5-7 minutes.

Return the mushroom mixture to the medium bowl. In a small bowl, whisk the eggs until blended and then stir into the mushroom mixture. Add the green onions, black rice, and panko and gently mix together. Form the mushroom mixture into 4 patties.

FOR THE PICKLED CARROTS

2 cups peeled and shredded carrots

1 jalapeño chile, stemmed and thinly sliced into rounds

1 cup water

½ cup white wine vinegar

½ cup rice vinegar

¼ cup sugar

Kosher salt

FOR THE BURGERS

1 lb mixed wild or cultivated mushrooms, such as shiitake and portobello, stemmed and brushed clean

3 tablespoons soy sauce

2 tablespoons rice vinegar

1 tablespoon Sriracha or other chile sauce

3 tablespoons toasted sesame oil

Preheat a stove-top grill pan over medium-high heat, or preheat an electric indoor grill on medium-high heat. Brush with canola oil.

Place the burgers on the grill and cook, flipping once, until nicely grill marked and a similar texture throughout, about 5 minutes per side. Transfer the burgers to a plate.

Meanwhile, make the smashed avocado: In a medium bowl, mash together the avocados and lime juice, and season with salt and red pepper flakes.

Place the buns, cut sides down, on the grill and cook until golden brown and crisp, about 1 minute. Transfer to a plate. Top each bun bottom with a burger, pickled carrots, and smashed avocado. Close with the bun tops and serve.

Serves 4

1 tablespoon minced peeled fresh ginger

2 cloves garlic, thinly sliced

2 large eggs

2 green onions, white and pale green parts only, sliced

2 cups cooked black rice

2 cups panko bread crumbs

Canola oil as needed

FOR THE SMASHED AVOCADO

2 avocados, pitted and peeled

Juice of 1 lime

Kosher salt

Red pepper flakes

4 sesame seed buns, split

Salmon Burgers with Fennel Slaw & Lemon-Caper Yogurt

The secret to great salmon burger texture is to grind half of the fish and chop the remainder. That combo, plus at least a half hour in the refrigerator, guarantees these moist, flavorful burgers won't fall apart during grilling.

To make the salmon burgers, cut half of the salmon into ¼-inch pieces; set aside. In a food processor, combine the remaining salmon, panko, yogurt, mustard, chives, dill, egg, lemon zest, 2 ½ teaspoons salt, and ½ teaspoon pepper and pulse until well combined. Transfer to a medium bowl and fold in the chopped salmon. Form the salmon mixture into 4 patties and refrigerate for at least 30 minutes or up to 2 hours.

Meanwhile, make the fennel slaw: In a medium bowl, stir together the fennel, parsley, vinegar, and olive oil. Season with salt and pepper. Set aside.

Preheat a stove-top grill pan over high heat, or preheat an electric indoor grill on high heat. Brush with canola oil.

Place the burgers on the grill and cook, flipping once, until nicely grill marked and an instant-read thermometer inserted into the center of the burgers registers 125°F for medium-rare, about 5 minutes per side, or until done to your liking. Transfer the burgers to a plate and let rest for 3 minutes.

Garnish the burgers with the reserved fennel fronds and serve with the fennel slaw.

Serves 4

FOR THE BURGERS

1 ½ lb skinless salmon fillets

½ cup plus 2 tablespoons panko bread crumbs

½ cup whole-milk Greek yogurt

2 tablespoons Dijon mustard

2 tablespoons each minced fresh chives and minced fresh dill

1 large egg

Grated zest of 1 lemon

Kosher salt and pepper

Canola oil as needed

FOR THE FENNEL SLAW

1 fennel bulb, trimmed and shaved on a mandoline, fronds reserved for garnish

½ cup fresh flat-leaf parsley leaves

2 tablespoons white wine vinegar

2 tablespoons olive oil

Kosher salt and pepper

Serve with lemon-caper yogurt: Combine ¾ cup Greek yogurt, 1 tablespoon chopped capers, and the zest and juice of 1 lemon, and pepper to taste.

Chicken Burgers with Lemon-Garlic Aioli & Arugula

For smaller bites, form the chicken mixture into 8 patties and pair them with 8 slider buns. If you're watching your carbs, skip the buns and wrap the burgers or sliders in aioli-slathered butter lettuce or romaine leaves.

To make the chicken burgers, in a food processor, combine the chicken, ricotta, Parmesan, onion, lemon zest and juice, rosemary, paprika, cayenne, and 1 teaspoon salt and pulse until the ingredients are combined and the chicken is blended. Transfer to a medium bowl. Using a rubber spatula, stir in the panko. Form the meat mixture into 4 patties.

Preheat a stove-top grill pan over medium-high heat, or preheat an electric indoor grill on medium-high heat. Brush with oil.

Season the tops of the burgers with salt and black pepper. Place the burgers, seasoned side down, on the grill and cook until nicely grill marked, about 5 minutes. Then season the tops of the burgers with salt and pepper. Flip the burgers and cook for 5 minutes. Flip the burgers again and cook for 2–3 minutes, then flip a final time and cook for 2–3 minutes longer until the burgers are cooked through. Transfer the burgers to a plate and let rest for 5 minutes. Spread the cut sides of the buns with the lemon-garlic aioli. Top each bun with a burger, tomato slice, onion slice, and a small handful of arugula. Add the bun tops and serve.

Serves 4

FOR THE BURGERS

1 lb skinless, boneless chicken thighs, cut into 2-inch cubes

¾ cup ricotta cheese

½ cup grated Parmesan cheese

½ cup diced red onion

Zest and juice of 1 lemon

2 teaspoons chopped fresh rosemary

½ teaspoon paprika

Pinch of cayenne pepper

Kosher salt and pepper

1 cup panko bread crumbs

Canola oil as needed

4 brioche buns, split

Lemon-Garlic Aioli, page 24

1 tomato, sliced

1 onion, thinly sliced

Arugula, for topping

Classic Beef Burger with Blue Cheese & Grilled Onions

Here is our favorite all-beef burger. Fat delivers flavor and moisture to the meat and prevents burgers from drying out on a hot grill pan, so buy ground beef that is 80 to 85 percent lean for the tastiest result. See following page for photo.

In a medium bowl, gently mix together the ground beef, mustard, Worcestershire sauce, 2 teaspoons salt, and 1 teaspoon pepper. Form the meat mixture into 4 patties. Let stand at room temperature while you cook the onion.

Preheat a stove-top grill pan over high heat, or preheat an electric indoor grill on high heat. Brush with oil.

Meanwhile, in a small bowl, toss the onion slices with enough oil to coat and season with salt and pepper.

Place the onion on the grill and cook, turning once, until charred and very tender, about 10 minutes per side. Return to the bowl.

Brush the grill with more oil if needed. Place the burgers on the grill and cook 4–5 minutes per side. An instant-read thermometer inserted into the center of each burger should register a minimum of 130°F for medium-rare. During the last 2 minutes of cooking, top the burgers with the cheese, dividing evenly. Transfer the burgers to a plate and let rest for 5 minutes.

Meanwhile, place the buns, cut sides down, on the grill and cook until golden brown, 30–45 seconds. Transfer to a plate. Spread the cut sides of the buns with mayonnaise. Top each bun bottom with a lettuce leaf, burger, and onion. Close with the bun tops and serve.

Serves 4

1½ lb ground beef

1 tablespoon Dijon mustard

1 tablespoon Worcestershire sauce

Kosher salt and pepper

1 large yellow onion, cut into ½-inch slices

Canola oil as needed

¼ lb blue cheese, crumbled

4 brioche buns, split

Mayonnaise, for serving

4 butter lettuce leaves

Pick your favorite blue cheese—try Gorgonzola, Roquefort, Cambozola, or Maytag—for topping this iconic burger. Don't like blue? Go with shredded Cheddar or Gruyère slices.

Grilled Porterhouse Steak & Balsamic Onions with Fresh Thyme

With buttery tenderloin on one side of the bone and beefier top loin on the other, a porterhouse has something to satisfy nearly every steak connoisseur. This is a big, thick cut—one steak typically weighs about 2 pounds—so get the grill smoking hot to deliver a good sear and a succulent finish.

Let the steak stand at room temperature for 30 minutes before grilling.

Preheat a stove-top grill pan over high heat, or preheat an electric indoor grill on high heat. Brush with canola oil.

Meanwhile, in a small bowl, stir together the onion and olive oil, and season with kosher salt and pepper. Season the steak generously with kosher salt and pepper.

Place the onion on the grill and cook, turning occasionally, until softened, about 10 minutes. Return the onion to the bowl, add the vinegar and thyme, and toss to coat.

Brush the grill with more canola oil, if needed. When the grill is smoking, place the steak on the grill and cook, turning once, until nicely grill marked and an instant-read thermometer inserted into the center of the steak, away from the bone, registers 130°F for medium-rare, about 6 minutes per side, or until done to your liking. Transfer the steak to a cutting board and let rest for 10 minutes.

Meanwhile, return the onion to the grill and cook, turning once, until charred and slightly caramelized, about 5 minutes.

Cut the steak into slices and transfer to a platter. Top with the onion and the accumulated juices from the cutting board, sprinkle with flaky sea salt and thyme, and serve.

Serves 2–4

1 porterhouse steak, about 2 inches thick

Canola oil as needed

1 purple onion, cut into 8 wedges

3 tablespoons olive oil

Kosher salt and pepper

¼ cup balsamic vinegar

2 tablespoons fresh thyme leaves, plus more for garnish

Flaky sea salt, for serving

If you don't have a cherry pitter, stem the cherries, then insert the pointed end of a pastry tip or chopstick into the stem end of each cherry, forcing the pit out the opposite end.

Grilled Cherries with Honey Yogurt & Sugared Almonds

Peak-season cherries—firm, plump, and juicy—are delicious grilled, their natural sugars quickly caramelizing on the hot pan. If you like, skip the honey yogurt and spoon the charred fruits over a scoop of vanilla, honey, or lemon custard ice cream.

In a small frying pan over medium-low heat, toast the almonds, stirring occasionally, until light golden brown and fragrant, about 4 minutes. Remove from the heat and sprinkle with the sugar and a pinch of salt. Stir until the sugar melts and the almonds cluster together. Transfer to a parchment-lined plate and let cool.

Meanwhile, in a bowl, stir together the yogurt, honey, and vanilla. Set aside.

Preheat a stove-top grill pan over medium-high heat, or preheat an electric indoor grill on medium-high heat. Brush with oil.

Place the pitted cherries on the grill and cook, turning once, until lightly charred and softened, about 10 minutes.

Spoon the honey yogurt into bowls. Top with the grilled cherries, garnish with the sugared almonds and whole cherries, and serve.

Serves 2-4

⅓ cup sliced almonds

1 tablespoon sugar

Kosher salt

2 cups whole-milk Greek yogurt

2 -3 tablespoons honey

¾ teaspoon vanilla bean paste or vanilla extract

Canola oil as needed

1½ cups pitted cherries

½ cup whole cherries, stems intact

Grilled Figs with Vanilla Bean Ice Cream & Balsamic Vinegar

Grilling figs deepens their flavor and concentrates their sweetness. Look for large, plump, firm yet ripe figs of any variety. Black Mission, Brown Turkey, and Calimyrna are popular choices. For the best flavor, select an aged balsamic vinegar from Modena—the best your pocketbook can afford.

Preheat a stove-top grill pan over medium-high heat, or preheat an electric indoor grill on medium-high heat. Brush with canola oil.

Meanwhile, lightly brush both sides of the figs with olive oil and season with a pinch of pepper.

Place the figs, cut sides down, on the grill and cook until softened and lightly browned, about 5 minutes.

Meanwhile, remove the ice cream from the freezer and let it soften.

Scoop the ice cream into bowls. Top with the figs and lightly drizzle with balsamic vinegar. Garnish with the basil, sprinkle with flaky sea salt, and serve.

Serves 4

Canola oil as needed

6 ripe fresh figs, halved lengthwise

Olive oil as needed

Freshly ground pepper

Vanilla bean ice cream, for serving

Balsamic vinegar, for drizzling

4 fresh basil leaves, thinly sliced

Flaky sea salt

Grilled Sourdough with Crème Anglaise & Mixed Berries

Put together an assortment of whatever berries look best in the market—strawberries, blackberries, blueberries, raspberries—for this pairing of summer fruit and crème anglaise. To give the rich, creamy custard sauce a citrus note, add 2 teaspoons grated orange zest to the pan with the milk.

To make the crème anglaise, rinse the inside of a nonaluminum saucepan with water and shake out the excess water. Pour in the milk, set over medium-low heat, and cook until small bubbles form around the edges of the pan, about 5 minutes.

In a small bowl, whisk together the eggs, egg yolk, and sugar just until blended. Gradually whisk in half of the hot milk, then pour the egg mixture into the pan. Set over low heat and cook, stirring constantly, until the mixture is thick enough to coat the back of a spoon and leaves a clear trail when a finger is drawn through it, 6–8 minutes. Do not allow it to boil.

Strain the mixture through a fine-mesh sieve into a bowl and stir in the vanilla. Cover with plastic wrap, pressing it directly onto the surface to prevent a skin from forming, and let cool. Refrigerate for at least 2 hours or up to 2 days.

Preheat a stove-top grill pan over high heat, or preheat an electric indoor grill on high heat.

Meanwhile, brush the bread slices on both sides with oil and season with salt.

Place the bread on the grill and cook, flipping once, until charred, about 3 minutes per side.

Transfer the bread to a platter and drizzle with the crème anglaise. Garnish with the berries and pistachios and serve.

Serves 4

FOR THE CRÈME ANGLAISE

2 cups whole milk

2 large eggs plus 1 large egg yolk, at room temperature

¼ cup sugar

1 vanilla bean, split lengthwise, seeds scraped and reserved, or 2 teaspoons vanilla extract

4 slices sourdough or other coarse country bread

Olive oil as needed

Kosher salt

2 cups fresh berries

¼ cup roasted pistachios, crushed

Maple-Spiced Grilled Apples with Sea Salt

Here, apple quarters are grilled in foil packets to contain their spiced maple flavoring and keep them from breaking apart. Serve this late-summer dessert in individual bowls, or offer it family-style, spooning the apples and their syrup into a big serving bowl and topping them with scoops of vanilla ice cream.

In a large bowl, whisk together the maple syrup, butter, cinnamon, ginger, and ¼ teaspoon kosher salt until smooth. Add the apples and stir to coat.

Cut four 12-inch squares of heavy-duty aluminum foil. Place 3 apple quarters in the center of each piece of foil and fold up the sides to make a packet. Spoon 2–3 tablespoons maple syrup mixture over the apples in each packet, then seal the foil tightly.

Preheat a stove-top grill pan over high heat, or preheat an electric indoor grill on high heat.

Place the foil packets on the grill and cook until the sauce is bubbling and the apples are tender when pieced with a knife, 25–30 minutes.

Meanwhile, remove the ice cream from the freezer and let it soften.

Transfer the apples and sauce to a serving bowl. Top with vanilla ice cream, sprinkle with flaky sea salt, and serve.

Serves 4

⅓ cup plus 2 tablespoons pure maple syrup

2 tablespoons unsalted butter, melted

2 teaspoons ground cinnamon

½ teaspoon ground ginger

Kosher salt

3 apples, quartered and cored

Vanilla bean ice cream, for serving

Flaky sea salt

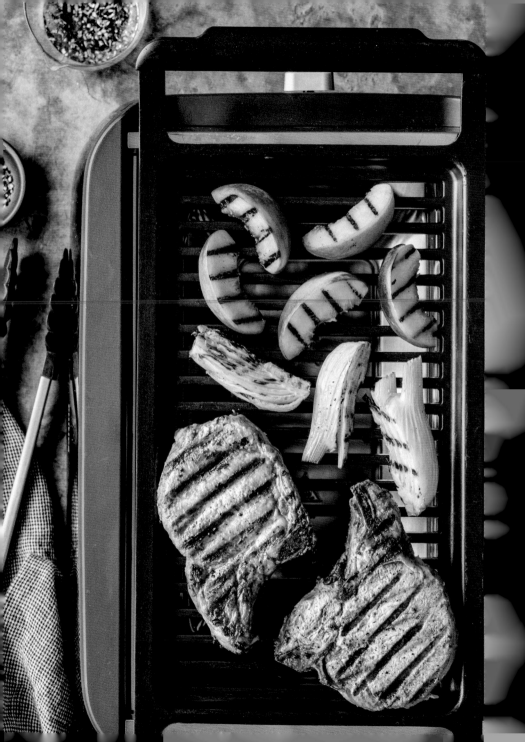

Index

Indoor Grilling

Conceived and produced by Weldon Owen International
in collaboration with Williams Sonoma, Inc.
3250 Van Ness Avenue, San Francisco, CA 94109

A WELDON OWEN PRODUCTION

P.O. Box 3088
San Rafael, CA 94912
www.weldonowen.com

Copyright © 2019
Weldon Owen International
and Williams Sonoma, Inc.

All rights reserved, including the right of
reproduction in whole or in part in any form.

Printed in China
10 9 8 7 6 5 4 3 2

Library of Congress
Cataloging-in-Publication data is available.

ISBN 13: 978-1-68188-509-4

WELDON OWEN INTERNATIONAL

President & Publisher Roger Shaw
Associate Publisher Amy Marr
Art Director Marisa Kwek
Designers Lola Villanueva & Lisa Berman

Managing Editor Tarji Rodriguez
Production Manager Binh Au
Imaging Manager Don Hill

Photographer Erin Scott
Food Stylist Lillian Kang
Prop Stylist Claire Mack

ACKNOWLEDGMENTS

Weldon Owen wishes to thank the following people
for their generous support in producing this book:
Josephine Hsu, Veronica Laramie, Rachel Markowitz,
Nicola Parisi, Elizabeth Parson, and Sharon Silva.